Sailing Camp

by Linda Lott
illustrated by Tom Newsome

Scott Foresman
is an imprint of

PEARSON

Glenview, Illinois • Boston, Massachusetts • Mesa, Arizona
Shoreview, Minnesota • Upper Saddle River, New Jersey

Illustrations
Tom Newsome

ISBN 13: 978-0-328-39360-2
ISBN 10:   0-328-39360-6

Copyright © Pearson Education, Inc. or its affiliate(s). All Rights Reserved.
Printed in the United States of America. This publication is protected by copyright and permission should be obtained from the publisher prior to any prohibited reproduction, storage in a retrieval system, or transmission in any form or by any means, electronic, mechanical, photocopying, recording, or otherwise. For information regarding permission(s), write to: Pearson School Rights and Permissions, One Lake Street, Upper Saddle River, New Jersey 07458.

Pearson and Scott Foresman are trademarks, in the U.S. and/or other countries, of Pearson Education, Inc. or its affiliate(s).

1 2 3 4 5 6 7 8 9 10 V010 17 16 15 14 13 12 11 10 09 08

It's the first day of sailing camp! Learning to sail can be fun. You wake up early to go to camp.

You will need to bring many things to camp. Bring sunglasses to protect your eyes from the sun. Bring a warm jacket in case it is cold.

Everyone on a boat needs a life jacket. You'll be getting one at camp. A life jacket will help you stay safe in the water.

You'll learn how to sail in the water. First you will learn about the parts of the boat.

sail

mast

deck

rudder

hull

You'll learn about water safety. Watch out for bad weather. Get back to land if there's a storm.

A sailboat moves when its sail is full of wind. You will be using the sail to catch the wind. Off you'll go!

You will learn how to move the boat. You will also learn how to tie it to the dock.

You have learned a lot about sailing. You must think about what you have practiced.

You raise the sail. The wind pushes it. You are sailing!

A sailboat is quiet. It doesn't scare away animals.

Keep your eyes open. You might see something wonderful!